Copyright

Written by: Miranda Crow

Publisher: Transcendence Publishing

Disclaimer

Dedication

To my wonderful hens

Table of Contents

Introduction

A wedding should be all about the love of a girl and a man for each other, however it's seldom a quiet and straightforward event. It's a giant celebration with its own traditions and requires months of preparation. Friends and relatives from far off will fly to witness the ceremony. Parents of one or two typically pay plenty of cash simply to create the marriage of their kids as unforgettable as possible. There are many pre-wedding events that are celebrated before the big day. Bachelorette's party for the bride and a bachelor's party for

the groom are like rituals of passage for the pair. A bachelorette's party became popular only recently, it should be fun, relaxed and involve plenty of drinks and partying.

This book contains no undeserving filler games or random ideas that are just added to fill up a book, unlike most other guides out in Kindle Store! This book was designed to be informative and fun.

I hope that you all have a really fun and great night!

This book will certainly make your Bachelorette Night at your Home a memorable one!

Enjoy!

Why celebrate your Hen Night at Home???

Oftentimes an evening with your best friends and loved ones is exactly what is needed. This Kindle Book will help make an evening just as special and more of an occasion than if you just hit the clubs and crawl around spending money and getting drunk! Lots of brides-to-be do not want to be dragged around the local bars being humiliated and made to kiss strangers and do dares! Who said that having your bachelorette party in your house can't be crazy and fun?

So if the thought of a night in surrounded by the ones you love, and enjoying some innocent fun sounds good then this is manuscript is for you. Or even use this guide to organize a pre going out get together at home before you hit the clubs!

Being frugal has never been more fashionable! There's no reason why you can't have a night to remember and not spend a small fortune!

What is a Hen Night?

A hen party is the celebration held before the wedding itself takes place. Normally, a week before to give the guests time to recover. They are attended by the bride-to-be and her female friends and family. The general idea is to celebrate the last moments of the bride-to-be's single life and offer her advice and support for her new married life she is about to embark on.

Definition from Dictionary:

Hen Night / Bachelorette Party:
Noun, British, Informal.

- *A celebration held for a woman who is about to get married, attended only by women.*

The word "hen" in the title is a reference to a female chicken. In the United States, the term is considered derogatory toward women in this time of sexual equality. In the past any gathering of women and girls might have been classified as a hen party. The meetings held by women have nothing to do with the innocent sewing bees of old, except for female bonding, there are more of a joyous celebration enjoyed by the future bride.

What Happens at a Hen Party?

The Bachelorette Party is usually planned by the brides' most closest friends, often the maid of honor or bridesmaids. Formally, the bride-to-be never hosts a party in honor of herself, although she may insist on participating in it's planning.

Whether the bride-to-be pays her share, or whether her share is divided between other participants is something to be determined by the organizers and the bride-to-be during the early stages of the planning process.

Participating in a bachelorette party is always optional. Many brides decline these parties because they fear they will be humiliated or will not enjoy this kind of fun. More traditional alternative is the bridesmaid's luncheon, hosted by the bride and/or her mother during the day, usually several days or a week before the wedding. A bachelorette's party is normally held in the evening, usually about a week (or at least a few days) before the wedding.

Unlike a bridal shower with young girls in attendance, the hen party is strictly for adult women.

Nowadays the Hen Party is aimed to cause a bit of blushing to the future bride. Her guests usually dress up the bride as a "noble" bride with joke shop items such as tacky plastic tiaras and veil, L-plates and other silly accessories! And she is generally made to look a bit foolish all in the name of good fun, but always with the aim being to give the bride-to-be a great night she will always remember. With a little humiliation and embarrassment thrown in for good measure, of course.

There are so many options for the many different kinds of entertainment, depending on what the organizers think will best please their guest of honor. While some see the idea of a bachelorette's party as a night of drunken debauchery, others see it as a chance for an opportunity for female bonding.

Bachelorette Party can be held in a public place, such as a restaurant, club or bar, or more commonly these days may be held in your very own home. The location often depends on the type or theme of your night. Some celebrations can get quite wild, with frenzied dancing and inappropriate behavior. So if you think your guests are going to be like thiss then consider your venue wisely. Alternatively, a day of drinking champagne at a day spa would be considered a tame version.

Other organizers choose a themed party, such as a "pamper party," with guests indulging in spa treatments, or maybe a Cooking themed night. It's very common to hire a male stripper, or a naked butler a popular Hen Party idea. He will wait on the guests serving drinks and food as well as hosting or taking part in hen party games and entertainment. This kind of entertainment obviously comes at a cost.

As we all know weddings can be very expensive so cutting the costs where you can is always a good idea. Which is why the idea of the Bachelorette Party at Home idea appeals to so many people.

I truly hope you enjoy this guide and that it'll give you everything you need and help to create a truly fantastic evening for the future bride and her loved ones.

Choosing a Theme

Having a certain theme to your night makes it so much fun and adds a sense of real occasion.

There is no reason why you can't dress up and have fun just because you're staying indoors!

Just think of all the fabulous photographs to be had!

Now I'm going to share with you the top themes that work really well for a Hen Night!

Top Theme Ideas to choose from:

Nurses, Minnie Mouse, Egyptian theme, Naughty Nuns, French Maids, Pirates, Super Hero theme, Cheerleaders, Angels, Naughty Secretary's, School Girls, seventies, Police Women (don't forget the handcuffs), Old Women - Great excuse to raid the charity shops, Fairies, Grease - The Movie, Vintage theme, Disney Princesses, Nautical, Bunny Girls, 1980's, Cowgirls, Glitz and Glamour, Dress as Men - Raid your partners wardrobe! Spice Girls, Sex in the City, Zombies - Really good fun and so popular at the moment!

Get some custom made shirts ! It's an awesome idea!

Different Food Ideas

Here's a Great Idea: Bake off fun.

Get the guests to bring some food in a cheeky design or bake. Get the bride to be to judge the winner with an ultimate taste off.

Cheeky Cookies! Or Naughty Cupcakes! Something Savoury?

When it comes to supplying food for your party you don't have to go spend a fortune.

It's totally down to your budget and how far you want to go.

If you want to impress others, you could hire a party catering firm to the supply food.

A much cheaper option is to use one of the big supermarkets to make you up some party platters for you to collect before hand.

You could hire a chocolate fountain! These work great for a Hen night, everyone will definitely remember that!

You don't have to lay on a full top notch Buffett! You could just order a Take Away! Just go easy on the poor unsuspecting Delivery guy!!

Or just agree with all the guests before the party to bring a little something along to contribute to the food, sweet. Friends and family are always more than happy to do this.

Another fun idea: You could get a rude novelty cake made. Most good novelty cake makers will happily make you a cake in the shape of a naked man or penis. Prices are around 70$.

If you are theming your celebration with the theme with the food and cake too. You can have so much fun with this, but remember drinks and food are only a small part of the wonderful entertaining evening ahead.

Decorations and Alcohol

It's time to have fun!

You can buy many varieties of hen night balloons, or if you want to be a bit saucier blow up some condoms and put those up around the house!

Of course if you have decided to theme the evening in a particular way then run with your theme!
It's so easy to get hold of great but reasonably priced decorations!

Use sites like Ebay or Amazon- simply type into the search bar "Bachelorette Night Decorations!"
You'll find **very** cheap and fancy decorations.

You can get anything from L-plate confetti to personalized balloons, banners, and inflatable men to penis straws! Invest more money in this. In my opinion, decorations *does matter*.

Cocktails, Alcohol!

There is a plenty of things you can do that don't involve alcohol on your bachelorette night - we think that more hen parties should be about celebrating your wedding with friends rather than getting drunk. Although, if you want to make things more interesting, you should consider investing money in good alcohol. It will make your celebration a very memorable one.

Few drinks on arrival always gets your guests in the right mood! Here are the best, most delicious and most popular drinks consumed on a hen night!!

Don't do anything that you will regret later. Always remember to drink responsibly.

My Top 10 Bachelorette Party Cocktails

1 - Woo Woo

1 part Vodka

1 part Peach schnapps

4 parts Cranberry juice

Ice

Sex it up - add a slice of peach to complete the look.

Basically a Sex on the Beach, minus the orange juice. A good one to make in bulk at parties because pretty much everyone likes it.

2 - Mojito

1 part Rum

0.5 parts Lime Cordial

3 parts Soda Water

A wedge of fresh lime

Ice

Sex it up - add apple liquor as well as rum to make an apple mojito

A Cuban drink that was apparently a favourite with the author Ernest Hemingway. The name means literally

'Something wet'.

3 – BJ, Blow Job

1 part whipped cream

1 part Kahlua

1 part Bailey's Irish cream

1 part Vodka

Instructions for drinking!

Layer in order into shot glass. Pick up the glass with your mouth! No hands allowed and tilt your head back shooting the creamy liquid down your throat!!

Always get a laugh!!

4 – Pornostar!

1.5oz Vodka

.5oz Blue Curacao

3oz Pineapple juice

1oz Coconut cream

splash of Malibu

Pour Vodka, Blue Curacao, pineapple juice and coconut syrup in a shaker full of ice. shake over ice strain into martini glass. add a splash Malibu over top of drink rim glass with fresh pineapple and garnish with an orange wheel

Great coloring and pretty to look at.

5 - Pimms

1 part Pimms

2 parts Lemonade

Sliced Apple, Lemon,

Orange and Cucumber

Sex it up - for some extra fizz mix with sparkling white wine instead of lemonade.

First created in 1823 by James Pimm in London, this drink is pretty much a British institution. So it would only be patriotic to enjoy a glass this summer.

6 – Bellini with Schnapps

1 part Peach Schnapps

1 part sparkling white wine

Sex it up - add Grenadine for a stronger splash of colour.

Originally from Italy, this cocktail gained its name because its colour resembled a toga-wearing figure in a painting by Giovanni Bellini.

7 - Red Headed Beauty

1 part Jagermeister

1 part Peach schnapps (archers)

1 part Cranberry juice

Sex it up with a shake & ice than strain into shot glass
Tastes great, real easy to make and drink.

8 - Slippery Penis

1 part Peppermint Schnapps

1 part Amaretto

Layer in shot glass

9 – Crazy Nymphomaniac

1 shot Spiced Rum

1/4 shot Peach Schnapps (archers)

1/4 shot Malibu

Shake with ice and strain into tumbler

10 - Orgasm

Bailey's Irish Cream - as much as you like!

2 parts Tia Maria

1 part Vodka

Ice

Whipped cream

1 part White Rum

Put 2/3 cubes of ice in a glass. Add 1 shot of vodka and 1 shot of white rum.

Then add the two shots of Tia Maria.

Quickly pour over the baileys and whisk briskly to combine all the spirits together.

Finally add some whipped cream on top to finish the cocktail off.

Male Strippers

When ordering a stripper online you are given a catalogue of men to choose from. Strippers come in all sizes and shapes and you can choose any theme you like. So if you have a fetish for a Fireman or maybe an Officer or Tarzan or even go for something a bit obscure like a dwarf stripper or and old man stripper you can choose! Remember the idea is to make the future bride suitably embarrassed!

There are hundreds of decent agencies out there if you wanted to all club together for the evening. The strippers can go as far as you are prepared to pay. So make sure you are clear upon booking as to exactly what kind of service you require!

For the classic Hen Party experience, hire a male stripper! Check with your guests, as some might be really offended.

Just because you haven't gone to a strip club it doesn't mean you can't bring the strip club to you. The sight of a man covered in baby oil cannot fail to get everyone in the group having fun, as well as giving them something to giggle about throughout the weekend.

To give you an idea of cost you can pay anything from $50 to $100 per hour.

Music – Sound of Life

Music is so important to when it comes to creating an atmosphere of excitement.

Keep in mind to be courteous to any neighbors. If you go and speak to them in advance and explain that you are having a hen party and that there could be some extra noise on a particular night generally people are very understanding and accept it.

The last thing you want is to hit them with a barrage of noise and giggles and for them to have no warning or be given the option to go out themselves. As long as the neighbors know why there is extra noise they generally don't seem to mind.

If you didn't want to speak them all face to face you can always use this note template and pop it through their door a week before.

Dear Neighbors,

My name is _____ and I live at_____.

I would like to notify you that on _____I will have a bachelorette's party at my home. The celebration may require us to use extra parking slots. There also will be music played. I would like to say sorry in advance for any disturbance, and assure you this will not be a regular occurrence.

I apologize for any inconvenience that we might cause, we will do everything to keep things reasonable and smooth. Thank you in advance for your understanding.

What kind of music should you play?

The answer to this question is very tricky. It would all depend on what kind of night you were planning on having. As you work your way through this book you would have already decided on a theme and style of hen party. This will reflect hugely what kind of music you wanted to play to set the right mood.

If you are strongly going with a particular theme then playing the right music will enhance your evening. For example, if you were going with a 1980s theme then the best thing to get is a 1980s party compilation cd. Or if you were going to have a more sophisticated evening and go with the glitz and glamour theme then something a little more classic would work.

But at the end of the day this is still a hen party and there are certain songs that are hugely associated with this. Here are just a few Hen Night Party Cds available for you to buy through retailers like EBay or Amazon.

This list will give you an idea of the kind of songs they include:

Dancing Queen' by Abba, 'Single Ladies' by Beyoncé, 'What a Feeling' by Flashdance, 'Crazy in love' by Beyoncé, 'I need a hero' by Bonnie Tyler, 'Valerie' by Amy Winehouse, 'Fame' by Irene

Cara,'I'm your man' by Wham, 'Hit Me Baby One More Time' by Britney Spears, 'Do you love me' by Dirty Dancing, 'Love Shack' by B52s, 'Like a Virgin' by Madonna, 'Just Dance' by Lady GaGa, 'Ooh ah just a little bit' by Gina G, 'Girls Just Wanna Have Fun' by Cyndi Lauper, 'Dancing Queen' by Abba, '(I've had) The Time of My Life' from Dirty Dancing. 'Bootilicious' by Destiny's Child, 'Lady Mamalade' by Christina Aguilera, 'Baby One More Time' by Brittany Spears, 'Fight for this Love' by Cheryl Cole, 'Do you Love me' from Dirty Dancing, 'Reach' by S Club 7, 'Push It' by Salt n Pepa, 'I'm So Excited' by The Pointer Sisters, 'You've Got To Love by Candi Staton, 'Hot Stuff' from Full Monty, 'Vogue' by Madonna, 'Crazy In Love' by Beyoncé, 'Sisters are doing it for themselves' by Aretha Franklin, 'Bad Romance' by Lady Gaga, 'Spinning Around' by Kylie.

Try to get everyone singing along and dancing around their handbag, all songs are suitable for all ages and some really classic tunes! The key is to get the songs that everyone might know!

Great! We have the decorations, the theme are up, the alcohol are ready the music is ready to go!! Don't forget about the snacks!

Let's have some fun!

But before the celebration there is something very important that needs to be done!

THE Bachelorette Party PLEDGE:

<u>Have to be taken by every participant!</u>

I solemnly swear that as a woman of the world I will respect and honor my sisters.

I will not reveal secrets of our evening.

I understand that violating this treatment will spread bad karma upon my being and may result in increased bloating and cramping.

If asked about the evening I shall reply:

I just had a good time!

Indoor Party Games!

Remember to tell everyone about the rules before starting any game!

This may involve printing out certificates and getting together some items for certain games.

You can add prizes to make the games more competitive.

We recommend bars of chocolate or miniature bottles of wine, condoms.

Keep the prizes simple and cheap!

Next you have a total of 14 games for you to play at home with your closest family and friends!

There are no restrictions on the number of players for any of the games!

You can have anything from 4-99.

Each game has been researched and played at bachelorette nights at home around the country with great feedback!

So you can play with family and friends.

Each game has been explained in detail in with very simple easy to understand instructions!

Each game tells you exactly what you will need in order to play it, and an explanation of the kind of game; for example a quiz, a physical or a drinking game, etc.

Let the fun begin!

Game 1:

Your True Destiny Game!

A great simple ice-breaker game, guaranteed to get everyone laughing!

<u>All you need is a piece of paper and a pen for each Hen!</u>

Give all the hens a piece of paper and a pen and get them to write the numbers 1 -13 down one side!

Get them to write down a one word answer to the following things!

1: A Place

2: A Colour

3: A Number between 1–15

4: A Smell

5: A Size (e.g. Small, large, Huge!)

6: A Number between 1-20

7: An Animal

8: A Number between 1-25

9: A Cartoon Character

10: A Rude or Insulting Name!

11: A Vegetable

12: A TV Show

13: An Emotion (e.g. Happy, Sad, Angry)

Everyone should have 13 things written on their piece of paper!

Now it is time to read out their true destiny!

Read out the following statements:

Get each hen to read out their corresponding answer!

1: You will meet the man of your dreams at?

2: His hair will be?

3: His height will be…?   ft tall!

4: He smelt of?

5: The size of his bum was?

6: His willy will be … " ? Long!!

7: In bed he will be like a?

8: The number of children you will have is?

9: His nickname will be?

10: His pet name for you will be?

11: When he is too tired for sex you will use a ….? to satisfy you

12: You will make your fortune appearing naked on?

13: You will spend your lives together feeling?

Game 3:

Bride Versus Mother of the Groom!

Who knows more about the Groom? Let's find out.

Each Contestant will need some paper and a pen.

VERY IMPORTANT:

You MUST give the question sheet to the Groom to complete BEFORE the Hen night.

Get him to complete his answers as honestly as possible.

And tell him he must NOT show his Bride-to-be.

And return the sheet to the host!

You can play this game in many different ways!

Or add more Contestants!

Or add more questions!

Sit the contestants playing in front of all the other Hens.

The host can read out the questions, one at a time, and get each contestant to

Secretly write down their answer.

Then get the contestants to turn around their answer together.

The Winner will be the contestant with the most points.

And will be declared The Groom's BIGGEST FAN.

Ok let's play!!

Answer as quickly as possible!

Do not show your Bride-to-be your answers.

1) Which secondary school did you attend?

2) What was your first job?

3) What shoe size are you?

4) What is your favorite alcoholic drink?

5) What size trousers do you wear?

6) What is your favorite food?

7) How much did you weigh when you were born?

8) Name your favorite film?

9) Who is your best friend?

10) Who is your favorite comedian?

11) What aftershave do you wear?

12) What was your favorite TV program as a child?

13) How do you have your coffee?

14) What was your first Pet and what was its name?

15) What attracted you to you bride-to-be on the night you met?

16) If you had the choice, what uniform would you like to see the bride-to-be dressed up   in?

17) What is your favorite sexual position?

18) If you were on 'Who Wants to be a Millionaire', who would your phone a friend be?

19) If you could be a superhero, who would it be?

20) What is your favorite part of your bride-to-be's body?

21) What would your bride-to-be say is the best bit about your body?

22) What is your bride-to-be's most annoying habit?

23) If you had to pick a famous person to play your bride-to-be in a movie about herself, who would it be?

24) What are you most likely to argue about?

25) Where did you go for your first date together?

26) If you could send one thing to room 101 what would it be?

27) If you could sleep with one celebrity who would it be?

28) What is your worst habit?

29) What was your favourite toy when you were little?

30) What would be your dream car?

The 30 Questions to ask the Contestants in:

Bride verses Mother of the Groom.

You can always add more questions!

1)   Which secondary school did he attend?

2)   What was his first job?

3)   What shoe size is he?

4)   What is his favourite alcoholic drink?

5)   What size trousers does he wear?

6)   What is his favourite food?

7)   How much did he weigh when he was born?

8)   Name his favourite film?

9)   Who is his best friend?

10)   Who is his favourite comedian?

11) What aftershave does he wear?

12) What was his favourite TV program as a child?

13) How does he take his coffee?

14) What was his first pet and what was its name?

15) What do you think first attracted him to his Bride to be, the first night you met?

16) What uniform would he like to see his bride-to-be dressed up in?

17) What is his favourite sexual position?

18) If he was on 'Who wants to be a Millionaire', who would his phone a friend be?

19) If he could be a superhero, who would he choose to be?

20) What is his favourite part of his bride-to-be's body?

21) What does he think you would say If you were asked, what is the best part of the Grooms body?

22) What does he say is his bride-to-be's most annoying habit is?

23) If he had to pick a famous person to play his bride-to-be in a movie about herself, which actress would he pick?

24) What does he think; he and his Bride, to be are most likely to argue about?

25) Where did you go for your first date together?

26) If he could send one thing to room 101 what would it be?

27) If he could sleep with one celebrity who would it be?

28) What is his worst habit?

29) What was his favourite toy when he was little?

30) What would be his dream car?

The Winner is the contestant with the most points!

Game 5:

Dressing the Bride!

Very fun and very creative game! For all you want-be designers out there!

You will need PER TEAM 1 x toilet roll, Sticky tape and silver foil!

Split your Hens into 2 teams!

Each team nominates one Hen to play the Bride!

Each team will have 10 minutes to use the toilet roll, sticky tape and silver foil to design, make a Wedding Dress, Tia and Jewellery and then dress the nominated bride!

When the time is up the Brides must parade their outfits to the other Hens, describing their designs like in a real fashion show!

Your aim is to design and make the best wedding dress possible with the materials you have available to you!

The REAL Bride-to-be can decide the winning team!

Get your Cameras at the ready for this one!

Game 6:

Most Beautiful Bra!

Another fun and very creative game! For all you want-to be designers out there!

You will need supermarket type carrier bags!! (thin with handles)

Split your Hens into teams of 2 or 3!

Each team nominates one Hen to play the Bride!

Each team will have 5 minutes to use only 2 carrier bags to design, make and then fit a bra onto the nominated bride!

You can do this over their clothes to avoid embarrassment!

So just rip, tie and fashion and attach to the nominated Hen!

When the time is up the Brides must parade their bras to the other Hens, describing their designs like in a real fashion show!

Your aim is to design and make the best bra possible using only the 2 carrier bags!

The REAL Bride to be can decide the winner!!!

Get your Cameras at the ready for this one too!!!

Game 8:

The Name Famous Game!

Another very simple to play game!

<u>All you will need is some alcohol and a basic spelling ability!</u>

One of the hens begins the game by saying the **first** and **last** name of someone famous.

The next hen says the name of a famous person whose name begins with the first letter of the last name of the previous famous person.

For example, if I say "**G**eorge **B**ush," the next player could say "**G**eorge **B**ernard." The following player could say "**B**ruce Willis. You got it.

If a hen says a famous person who's first and last names begin with the same letter, the direction reverses!!!!!

The drinking happens when a Hen can't immediately rattle off a name!!

The Hen then must continue to **drink her drink without stopping** until she comes up with a name.

It's harder than it sounds—especially under pressure and the influence of alcohol!

Game 9:

Don't show teeth!

This game is hilarious especially after a few drinks!

<u>**Nothing needed to play!**</u>

To win simply be the last one in the game who hasn't shown their teeth.

You have to play the entire game without showing your teeth. If, at any point throughout the game, you show your teeth **YOU ARE OUT.**

Choose a subject from the list below: You then take it in turns to go around the circle and call out a word related to that subject. You must be quick with your answer and you must hesitate, stutter, laugh or repeat a word that has already been used or you are out!

What makes this game interesting is that you can't show your teeth at any point (which you do by pulling your lips over your teeth).
If you do happen to show your teeth and get caught by anyone, you alert the group by screaming "teeth, teeth" and flapping your arms at the player like wings.

(Make sure you don't show your teeth in the process!).

Played with the right group of people, this is an absolutely hilarious game.

List of Ideas for Subjects to choose from:

Sex
Films
Health related
Parts of the Body
Famous People
Wedding Day and others…..

This game is also played regularly on the hit TV show "Celebrity Juice"

It is the game that seems to cause the most laughter and guests at my party have been known to quickly run to the loo from laughing so much!!

Definitely one of my favorites!

Game 11:

The Balloon alley

This is a physical game

All you will need is long modelling balloons & pump and 2 of the Balloons!

Inflate a balloon for each team!

Split your friends into 2 equal numbered teams!

Play some fun at tacky music in the background too get you in the mood!

Get them to stand up in a line all facing the same direction!

Get the Hen at the start of the line to place the balloon between her legs, so that the balloon is sticking out at the front!

Now when both teams are ready! The Hen at the start of the line must pass the balloon to the Hen next to her. The Hen can receive the balloon anyway she wants without using her hands!! *(Through the legs!)*

Once the Hen has received the balloon she must then turn and pass the balloon to the next Hen in the line and so on! The winning team is the team that get their balloon to the end of the line, then all the way back to the start again!

But you <u>should not</u> use your hands at any time during the pass!

If the balloon is dropped it MUST be passed back to the start! And that team must start all over again! *Small hint - don't drop it!*

But NO HANDS allowed!

Get in line! Grab a balloon, Start the music and let's play The Balloon Pass!

Game 12:

Naughty Balloons

<u>All you will need is the modelling balloons balloons with pump and a creative flair!</u>

Blow up ALL the remaining modelling balloons using the pump!

(Leave about 2" Un inflated in each balloon so you can model and twist them with ease!)

-

Put them all into the middle of the Hens!

The idea of the game is to make a Balloon Model using the balloons of something Rude!!

Male or Female!!

The Hens can grab as many balloons as they can to make their balloon model!

To make it more fun, start a stopwatch, and give the Hens only 2 minutes to complete their art work!

The Bride-to-be judges the Winner!

Added Quitting!

The Hen who makes the Worst Balloon Model of the Night must be made to wear the Best Balloon Model of the night on their head!

(Secure with string! Or if you're feeling really creative make a hat with the remaining balloons!)

Game 13:

Bride Blushing Balloons

This game can start at the beginning of the night and be played at random intervals throughout the party.

 You will need is a pack of regular round balloons and some paper and some pens.

Get all the guests to jot down very humiliating questions for the Bride-to-be on bits of paper, roll them up and stick them into balloons, then blow up the balloons with the question inside.

Throw the balloons up from time to time and have the bride-to-be to pop a balloon, read aloud the questions, and answer it.

If she refuses to answer out of embarrassment, she has to drink a shot! Keep going throughout the night until every balloon has been popped and every question has been answered.

The more brazen the questions, the more fun this game will end up being!

And the more naughty the questions the drunker the Bride-to-be becomes!

You can always play this game with all the hens and nominate a hen to pop a balloon and answer the questions too.

*Share the **embarrassment**!*

Game 14:

The Secret Peg Game!

This game is for if you go out and about or to be used during the Wedding Reception!

This is the most fun you will ever have with a laundry related product Guaranteed!

<u>You will need a pack of fun coloured pegs!</u>

This game is to be played when your hens are out and about! A restaurant, pub, bar, club or even at the wedding reception itself!

This game is awesome folks!

Simply give a few pegs to each Hen! Their task is simply to get rid of their pegs by the end of the night! But there's a twist!

THEY MUST PEG A MAN!!!

They have to put their peg on the man that they feel is **HOT STUFF!**

Although,

They have to be so discreet! <u>The chosen man must NOT notice you do this!</u>

This is a hilarious game to observe!

Hens can peg the same guy more than once if he is in fact the hottest guy.

Watch your friends sneaking up on guys trying to peg them without being caught. And if they are caught watch them try and explain why they are trying to put a peg on their shirt. And by the end of the evening it's so funny to witness random guys walking around with pegs hanging from their shirts.

Thinking they look so cool! Unaware they have been **PEGGED!!!!!**

To make it more competitive give each hen a different coloured peg or get a pack of stickers to individualise the pegs for each hen.

That way you can see who's been pegging who.

Bride to be Souvenirs of the Hen Night

After all the fun of the night and all the alcohol that has been consumed and games that have been played I'm sure your hens are not looking as hot as when they first arrived!

As your guests arrive all dressed up, their hair and make up looking lovely. (unless of course you went for the zombie theme)

Take a photo of them individually holding a card with their name or role in the Wedding day.

Then at the end of the night take another photo of them holding the same card in the same position!

Make a montage of all the pictures in one frame!

These make hilarious keepsakes!

Maybe something a little less embarrassing get you hens to seal your night with a kiss.

Get a plain white canvas and get each guest to kiss it with red lipstick on and sign her name underneath the kiss.

Makes a great girlie modern art piece and keepsake!

Symbolize kissing the single life goodbye!

Huge Thank You and Words of Gratitude!

First and foremost, Thank You for downloading this book. At the end of the day I'm **extremely** grateful for **every** download and **every** purchase. It really makes me smile and motivates me. I wish that every person would put their best forward for the human race. I wish you unlimited mental strength and discipline to achieve your goals and dreams. **Together** we can make the difference.

If you found the information useful I would be extremely grateful if you could write a short Amazon review. It really does make the difference and I personally read every review and take notes. I want to improve my books, so that I can provide more value to other people. I know that my future books will give you the best experience possible.